Smile!
A Trip to the Dentist

Addition Facts

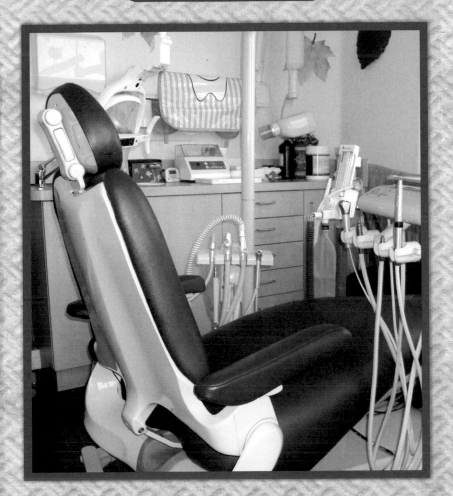

Loren I. Charles

Publishing Credits

Dona Herweck Rice, *Editor-in-Chief*; Lee Aucoin, *Creative Director*; Don Tran, *Print Production Manager*; Sara Johnson, *Senior Editor*; Jamey Acosta, *Assistant Editor*; Neri Garcia, *Interior Layout Designer*; Stephanie Reid, *Photo Editor*; Rachelle Cracchiolo, M.A.Ed., *Publisher*

A special thanks to the office and staff of Melba Mayes, D.D.S., M.S., pediatric dentist, Chino Hills, CA.

Image Credits

cover Stephanie Reid; p.1 Stephanie Reid; p.4 Stephanie Reid; p.5 Stephanie Reid; p.6 Stephanie Reid; p.7 Stephanie Reid; p.8 Stephanie Reid; p.9 Stephanie Reid; p.10 Stephanie Reid; p.11 Michael Ledray/Shutterstock; p.12 Stephanie Reid; p.13 Stephanie Reid; p.14 Stephanie Reid; p.15 Stephanie Reid; p.16 James Steidl/iStockphoto; p.17 Stephanie Reid; p.18 Stephanie Reid; p.19 jackhollingsworthcom, LLC/Shutterstock; p.20 Stephanie Reid; p.21 Stephanie Reid; p.22 (top left) Christophe Testi/Shutterstock, (bottom left) Iurii Konoval/Shutterstock, (right) Blue Lemon Photo/Shutterstock; p.23 UKRphoto/Shutterstock; p.25 (top left) Edyta Pawlowska/Shutterstock, (top right) Alex Staroseltsev/Shutterstock, (middle) Lepas/Shutterstock, (bottom) Matthew Cole/Shutterstock; p.26 Cammeraydave/Dreamstime; p.27 Stephanie Reid

Teacher Created Materials

5301 Oceanus Drive
Huntington Beach, CA 92649-1030
http://www.tcmpub.com
ISBN 978-1-4333-0418-7
©2011 Teacher Created Materials, Inc.

Table of Contents

Going to the Dentist

My cousin, Jaden, was going to a new **dentist** for the very first time.

She had lots of questions. So I told her what it is like.

First, you will meet the dentist.

You get to sit in a big chair. The chair tips back so the dentist can look in your mouth.

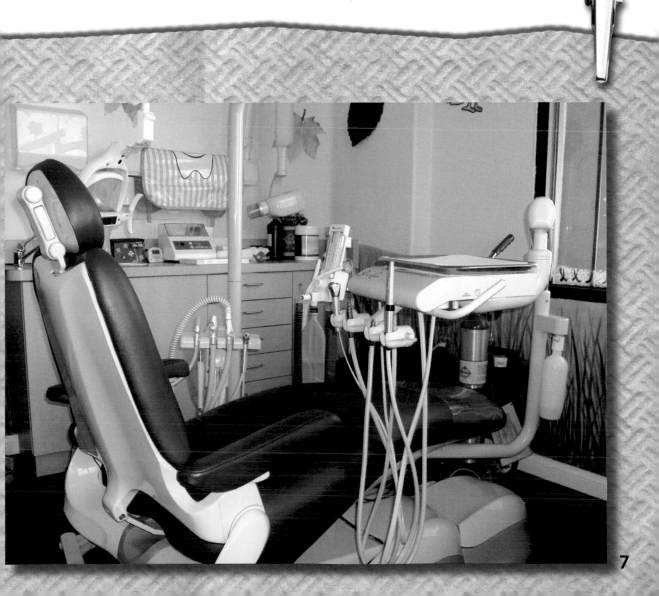

The dentist looks inside your mouth. She checks your tongue. She feels your cheeks and gums.

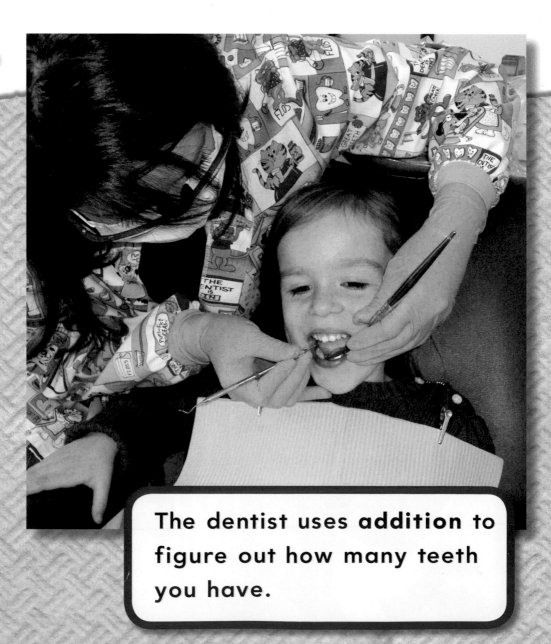

The dentist uses **addition** to figure out how many teeth you have.

She uses tools to look in your mouth. She wants to be sure everything is healthy.

LET'S EXPLORE MATH

By the time you are 2 or 3 years old, you have all of your baby teeth. Look at the picture below. Then answer the questions.

a. How many teeth are on the bottom?

b. How many teeth are on the top?

c. How many teeth are there altogether?

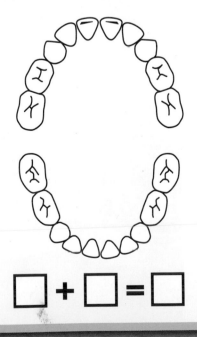

☐ + ☐ = ☐

The dentist may take **x-rays** of your teeth. X-rays are pictures of your bones.

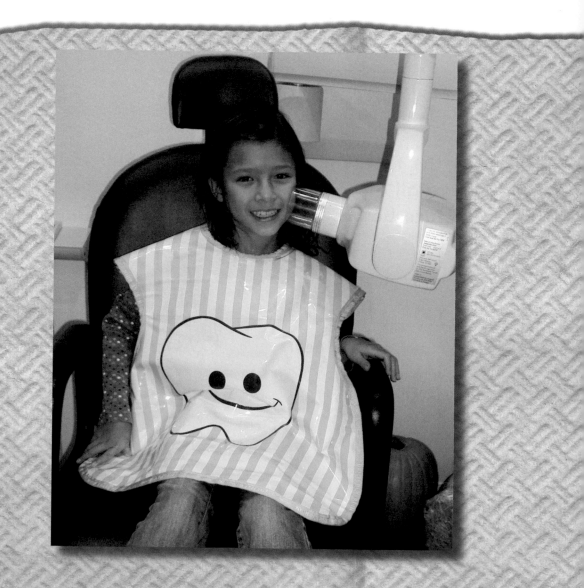

The x-rays show the dentist if your teeth have problems.

LET'S EXPLORE MATH

Elisa lost 3 teeth in 1st grade. She lost 4 teeth in 2nd grade. How many teeth did she lose in all?

☐ + ☐ = ☐

Next the dentist uses a scaler to scrape off the **plaque**. Plaque is sticky. It is not good for your teeth.

Then she polishes your teeth.

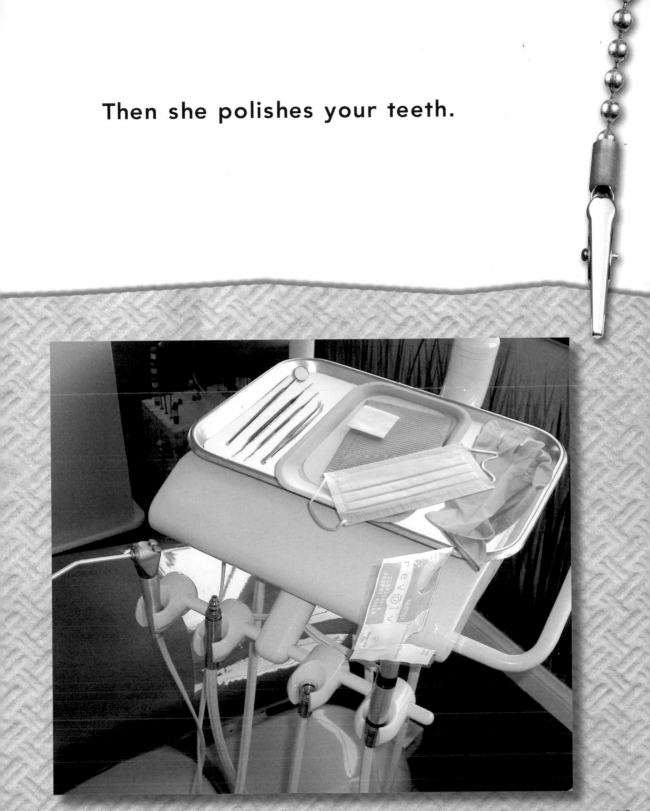

A Final Check

Now your x-rays are ready. The dentist checks them.

Then she looks inside your mouth.
She tells you about what she sees.

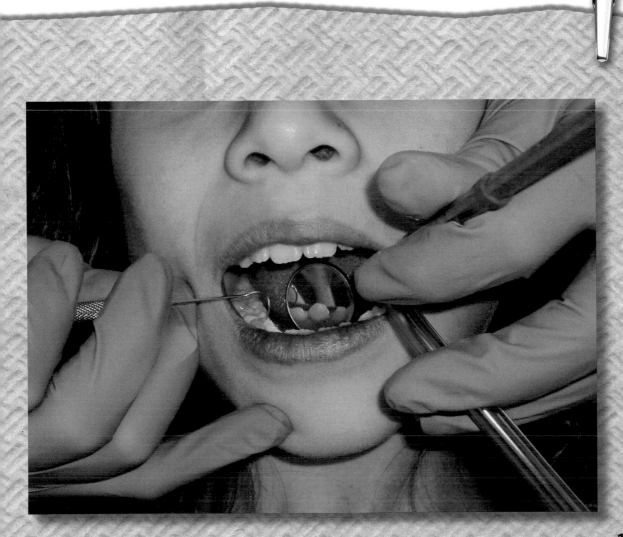

The dentist checks for a **cavity** in each tooth. A cavity is a soft part on a tooth.

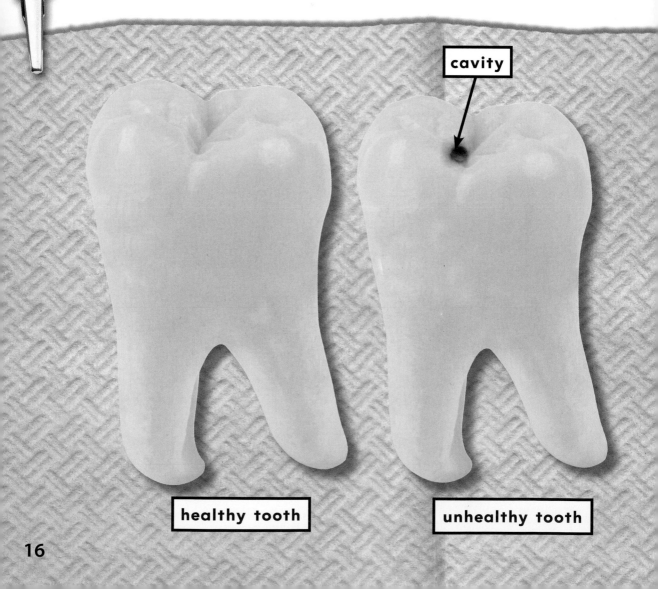

cavity

healthy tooth

unhealthy tooth

The dentist may find a cavity. You would need to come back to get it fixed.

LET'S EXPLORE MATH

The dentist found 1 cavity in Jaden's bottom teeth. The dentist found 2 cavities in Jaden's top teeth. How many cavities did the dentist find?

☐ + ☐ = ☐

The dentist also looks at how your teeth work when you bite down.

Someday you may need **braces**.
They help your teeth line up right.

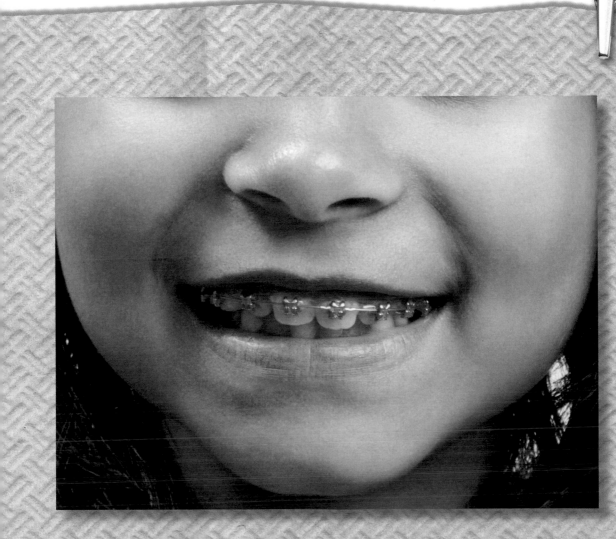

Brush and Floss

The dentist will show you the right way to brush and **floss**.

Flossing cleans between your teeth. It helps keep your gums healthy, too.

LET'S EXPLORE MATH

In the morning Jaden spends 4 minutes brushing and flossing. In the evening she spends 4 more minutes brushing and flossing. How many minutes does she spend brushing and flossing each day?

The dentist may tell you about foods that are bad for your teeth.

She may show you a chart like this. The foods in the chart can cause problems. Brush your teeth after eating them.

Sugary Foods
soda
candy bars
jam
syrup
gum with sugar
cookies
donuts

Some foods are good for your teeth. The dentist may tell you to eat the snacks in this chart.

Foods That Are Good for Teeth
popcorn without butter
kiwi
cheese
celery
carrots
nuts without salt
pretzels with low salt
cereal without sugar

They taste good. And they keep
your teeth healthy!

The dentist may give you a new toothbrush and floss when you are done.

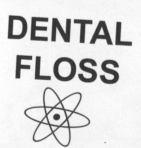

DENTAL
FLOSS

The best gift of all is a healthy smile!

Happyville Helpers

There are many people who work in a community. They all have special jobs. Their jobs help the people in the community.

Happyville is a very small town. The chart below shows some of the jobs that people have. It also shows how many people work at those jobs. Use the chart to answer the questions.

Community Helpers	Number of Workers
grocers	|||
sanitation workers	||
dentists	|
firefighters	||||
librarians	|
police officers	||||
doctors	|||
lawyers	||

a. Altogether, how many grocers and firefighters work in Happyville?

b. Altogether, how many sanitation workers and dentists work in Happyville?

c. How many community helpers work in Happyville?

Solve It!

Use the steps below to help you solve the problems.

Step 1: Use the chart to find the number of grocers and firefighters.

Step 2: Add those numbers together.

Step 3: Use the chart to find the number of sanitation workers and dentists.

Step 4: Add those numbers together.

Step 5: Add all of the tally marks together to find the total number of community helpers in Happyville. Try to make groups of 10. Then add the groups of 10s together.

Glossary

addition—the process of joining 2 or more numbers together to make 1 number called the sum

braces—wires that help make teeth straight

cavity—a soft or rotten part of a tooth

dentist—a doctor that takes care of teeth

floss—a special kind of thread used to clean between teeth

plaque—sticky stuff on teeth that can cause cavities

x-rays—special pictures of teeth or bones

Index

Let's Explore Math

Page 9:
a. 10 baby teeth
b. 10 baby teeth
c. 20 baby teeth

Page 11:
7 teeth

Page 17:
3 cavities

Page 21:
8 minutes

Solve the Problem

a. 7 community helpers
b. 3 community helpers
c. 20 community helpers